Color, Cut & Fold
OCEAN ANIMALS

PRACTICE SCISSOR SKILLS!

Let's get started!

All you need is a pair of scissors, a glue stick, and markers, colored pencils, or crayons! There are stickers to add to your creations when you have finished.

①

②

③ Start at the dot.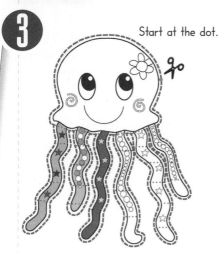

Carefully pull out the page you want along the perforation.

Color both sides of the page with markers, pencils, or crayons.

Starting at the dot, cut out the picture around the dashed line.

Cut around dashed lines.

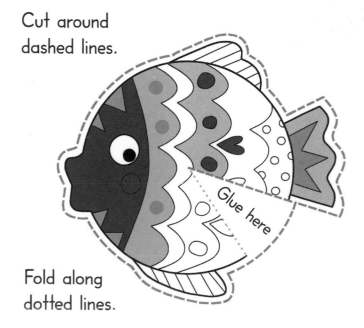

Glue here

Fold along dotted lines.

Where to cut?

- - - - - - - - - -

Cut along dashed lines like this.

Where to fold?

· · · · · · · · · · · · · · · ·

Fold along dotted lines like this.

Where to glue?

Some of the animals should be folded and glued. Follow the instructions on each page.

Shark

There are more than 400 types of sharks! Their babies are called pups.

1. Color the front and back of the shark.

2. Start cutting at the dot.

3. Fold the shark in half, and then cut along the dashed line at the center of the mouth.

4. Unfold, and then find
   stickers to decorate
   your shark.

Dolphin

Dolphins are very smart,
and they love to play.

1. Color the front and
   back of the dolphin.

2. Start cutting at the dot.

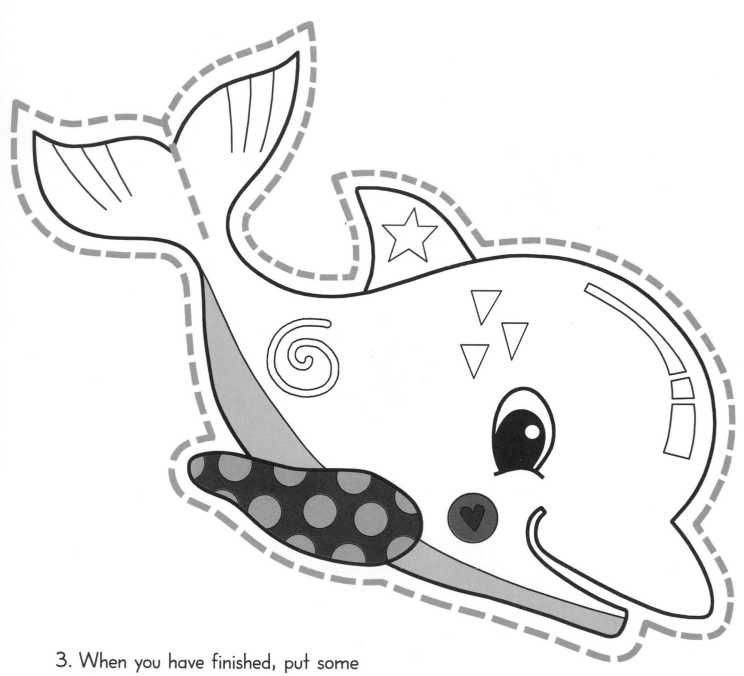

3. When you have finished, put some
   stickers on your dolphin!

Sea Turtle

Sea turtles can live
for over 100 years!

1. Color the front and back
   of the sea turtle.

2. Start cutting at the dot.

3. Fold all of the dotted lines toward the back of the turtle.

4. Glue each tab marked "Glue" under the next flap to make your sea turtle stand up.

Jellyfish

Some jellyfish glow
in the dark.

1. Color the front and
   back of the jellyfish.
2. Start cutting at the dot.

3. Fold the tentacles along the lines like an accordion.

4. If you want, you can attach a piece of thread to the head and hang your jellyfish.

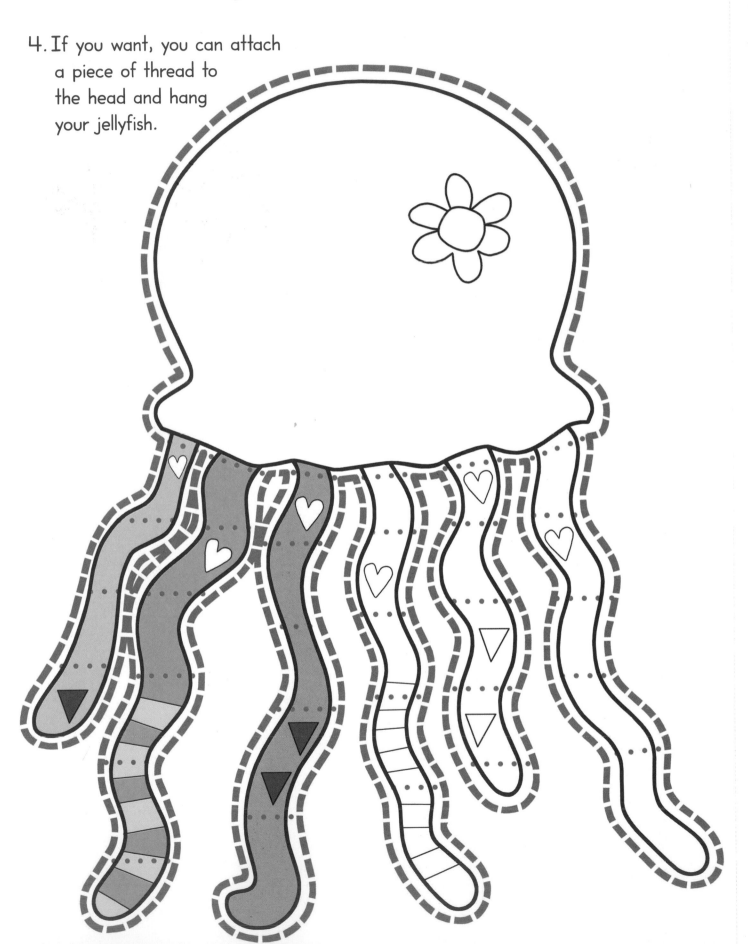

Hermit Crab

Hermit crabs like to decorate their seashell homes with things they find in the ocean.

1. Color the front and back of the hermit crab.

2. Start cutting at the dot.

3. Stick the triangular area under the flap with glue.

Glue

Glue

4. When you have finished, fold the shell to make the horns stand up.

! Ask a grown-up to cut around the head and horns!

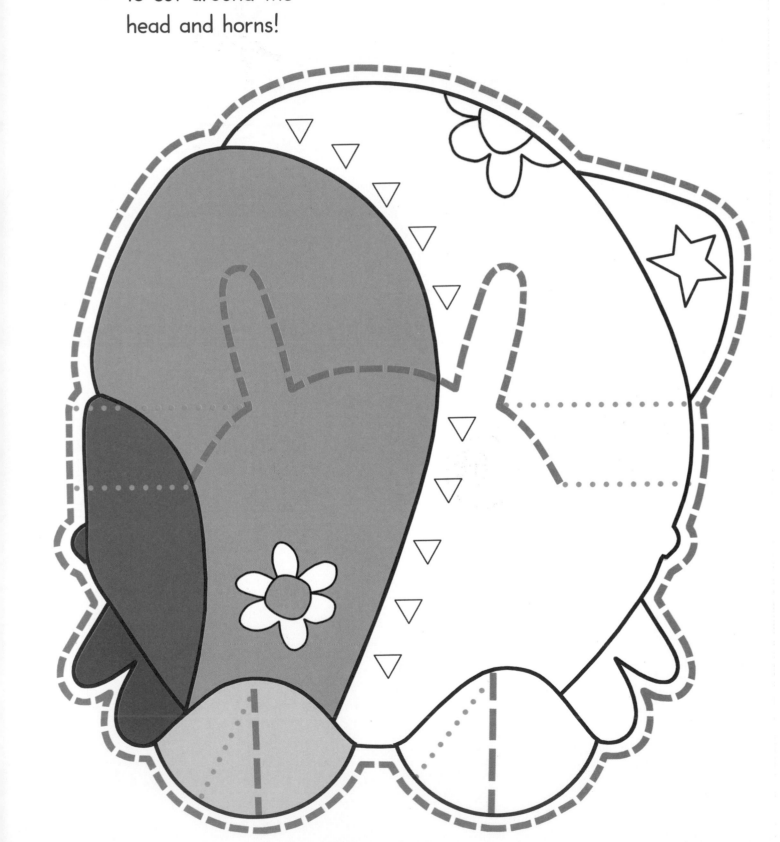

Starfish

Starfish aren't really fish. They are related to sea urchins.

1. Color the front and back of the starfish.

2. Start cutting at the dot.

3. When you have finished, fold
   along the dotted lines to make
   your starfish stand up.

Angelfish

Marine angelfish often live in coral reefs.

1. Color the front and back of the angelfish.

2. Start cutting at the dot.

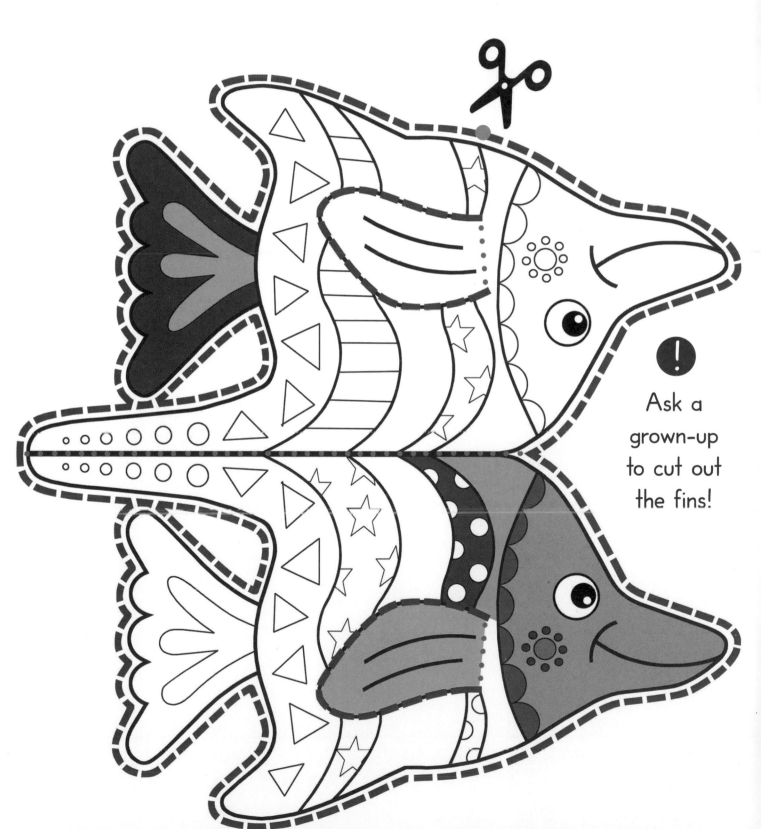

Ask a grown-up to cut out the fins!

3. Fold the angelfish in
   half, and fold out
   the side fins a little.

Lobster

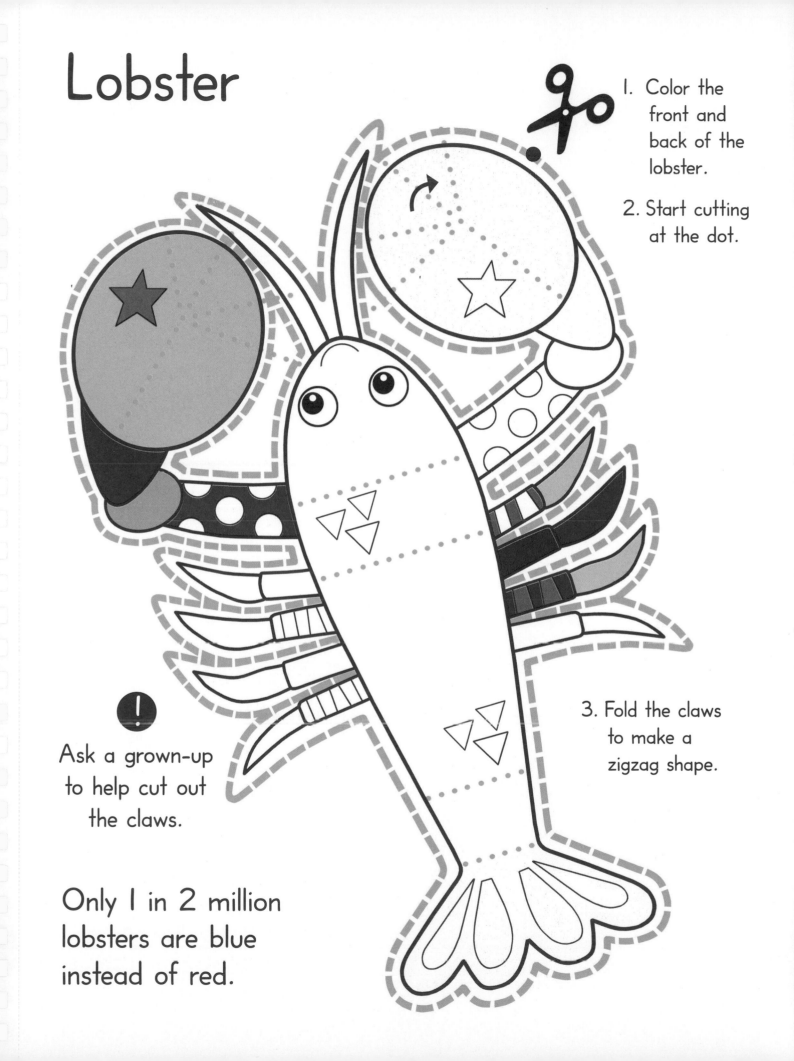

1. Color the front and back of the lobster.

2. Start cutting at the dot.

3. Fold the claws to make a zigzag shape.

Ask a grown-up to help cut out the claws.

Only 1 in 2 million lobsters are blue instead of red.

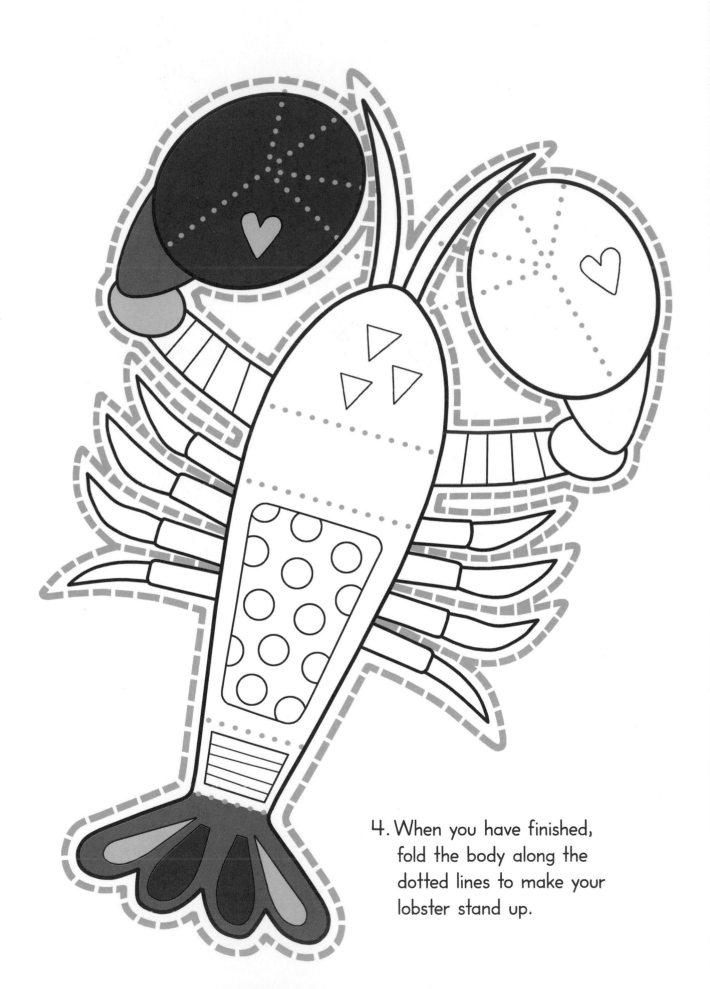

4. When you have finished, fold the body along the dotted lines to make your lobster stand up.

Seashell

Animals called mollusks live in seashells.

1. Color the front and back
   of the seashell.

2. Start cutting at the dot.

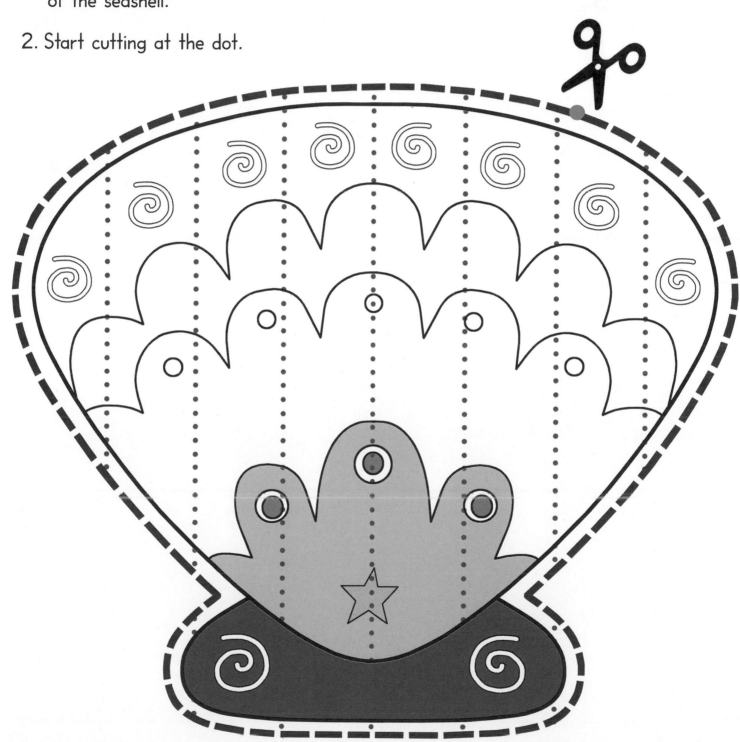

3. Fold along the dotted lines
   like an accordion. Unfold to
   make your seashell stand up.

Seahorse

1. Color the front and back of the seahorse.

2. Start cutting at the dot.

Seahorses like to swim in pairs with their friends.

3. Stick the triangle under the flap with glue.

Glue

4. If you want, you can attach a piece of thread to the head and hang your seahorse.

Octopus

An octopus has three hearts and eight legs.

1. Color the front and back of the octopus.

2. Start cutting at the dot.

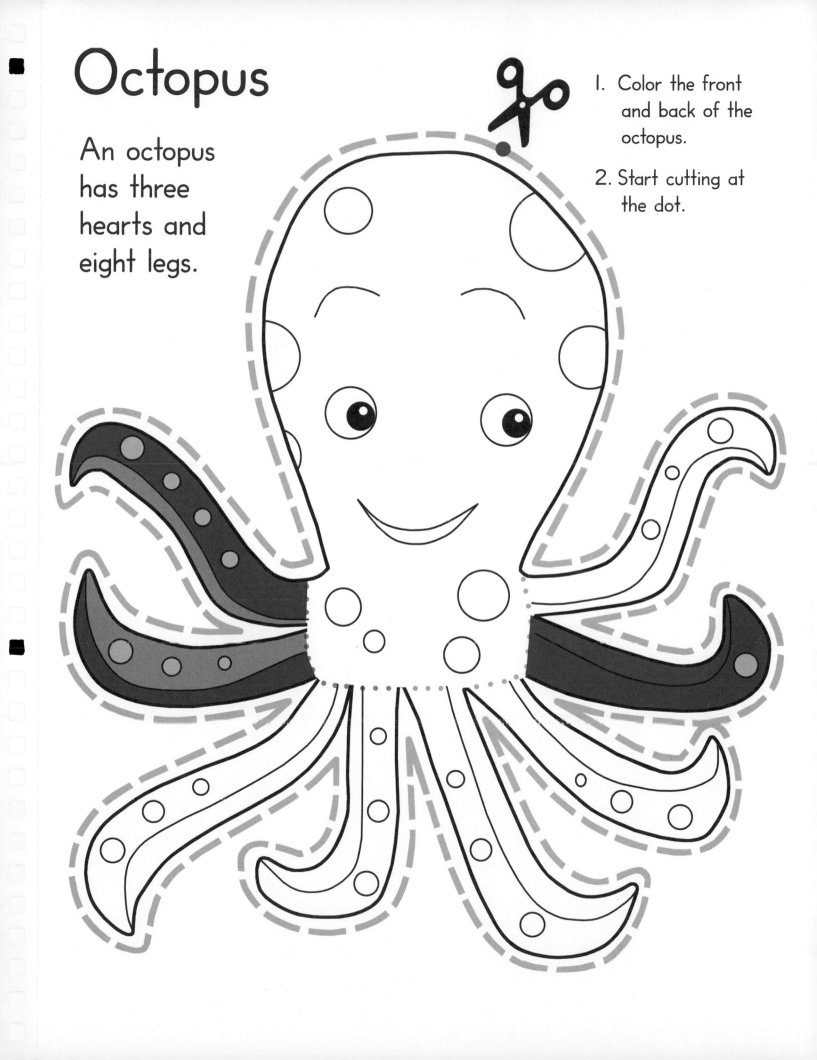

3. When you have finished, fold the legs a little, and tape your octopus to a window.

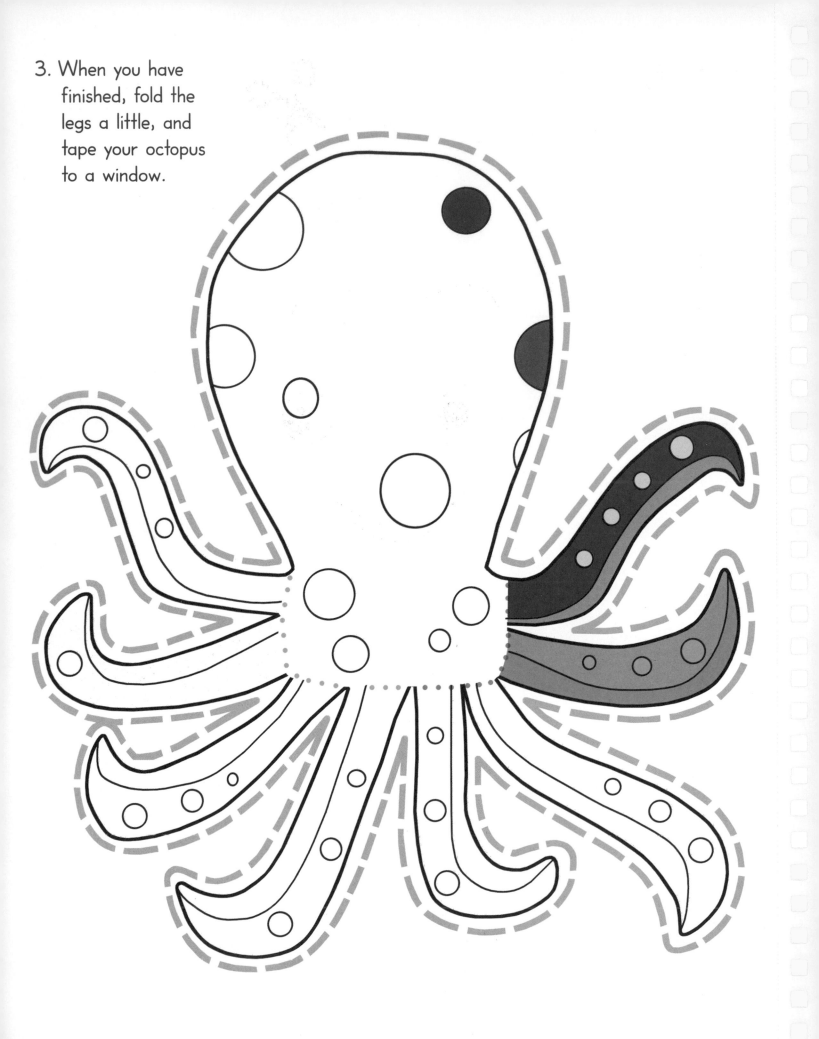

Fish

1. Color the front and back of the fish.

2. Start cutting at the dot.

3. Stick the triangle under here with glue.

Fish have gills that let them breathe underwater.

4. When you have
   finished, add
   some stickers!

Parrotfish

Parrotfish clean coral by nibbling at its surface.

1. Color the front and back of the parrotfish.

2. Start cutting at the dot.

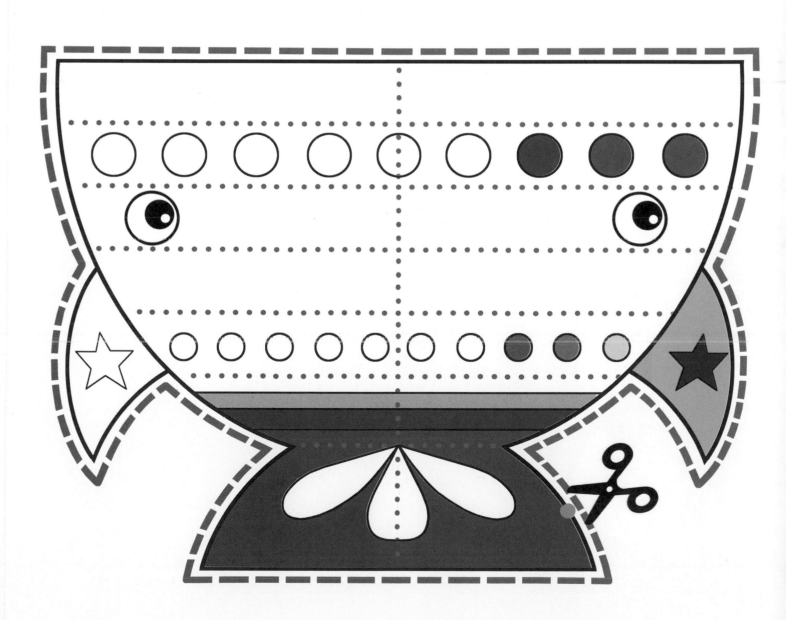

3. Fold the horizontal lines first, like an accordion.

4. Unfold a little, and then fold in half along the center dotted line.

5. Glue the inside together along the blue bar.

Penguin

Penguins can't fly, but
they can swim really well.

1. Color the front
   and back of
   the penguin.

2. Start cutting
   at the dot.

3. Fold in half,
   and then cut
   the beak.

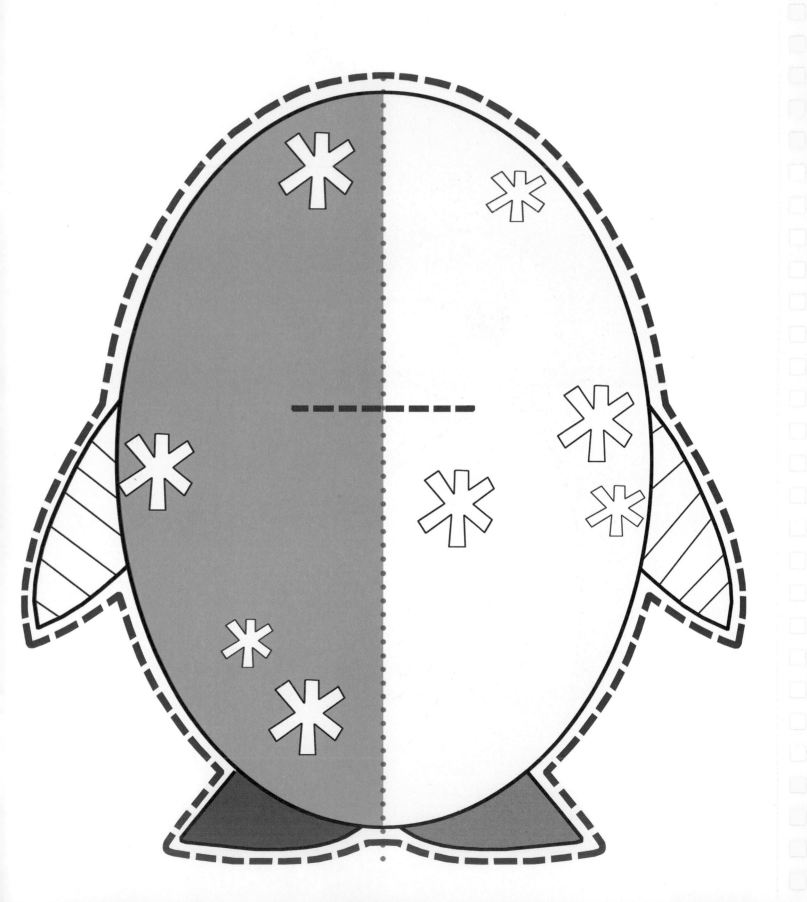

Whale

The blue whale is the largest animal in the world.

1. Color the front and back of the whale.

2. Start cutting at the dot.

3. Glue the triangle section marked "Glue" under the flap.

Glue

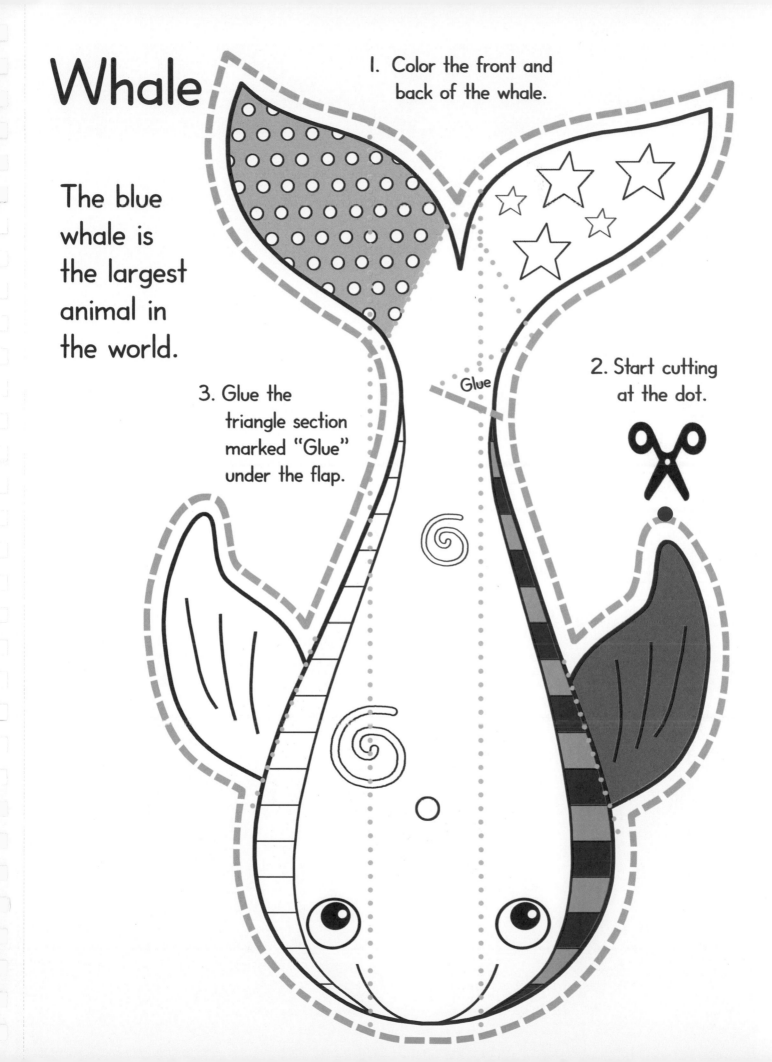

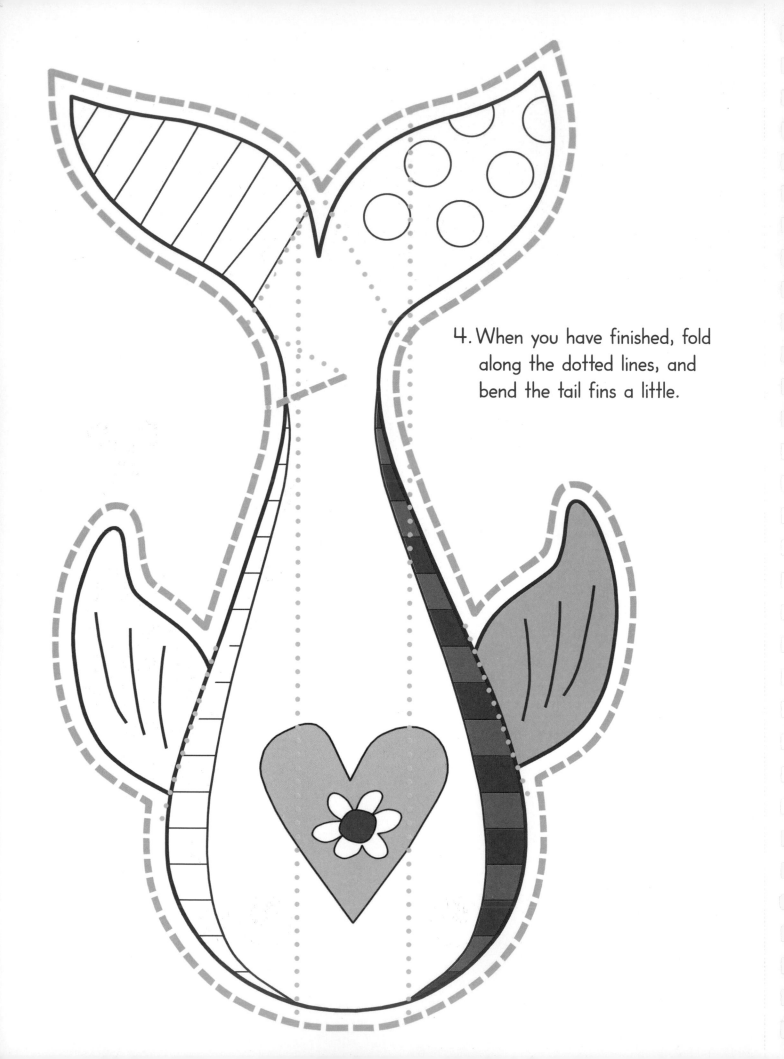

4. When you have finished, fold along the dotted lines, and bend the tail fins a little.